# Mama Bear Baby Bear

## A Native American Lore

Story By

## Linda Silvas

"Little Tree"

Third Printing

ISBN 978-0-9771720-0-9

All inquires should be addressed to:

Little Tree Creations
PO Box 178
Carlsborg, WA 98324

Toll Free 1-888-224-7039

www.MamaBearBabyBear.com
ltcreate@olypen.com

Printed in Korea

Printing facilitated by:
Star Print Brokers, Inc.
www.StarPrintBrokers.com

# Definition
of some of the backward words in this story.

Sgurd ....... (su gard) ............. drugs.

Tserofnair ... (Tes sir of nair) ..... Rainforest.

Noitalosi ..... (Know it al soe) ...... Isolation.

Skrof ........ (Forks) .............. Forks.

Yobdab ...... (Yo dab) ............ Badboy.

Lrigdoog ..... (El rig dog) .......... Goodgirl.

Cipmylo ..... (Sip my low) ......... Olympic.

Edutitta ..... (Ed u tude d a) ...... Attitude.

Elbuort ...... (El bort) ............. Trouble.

Regnad ...... (Reg nad) ........... Danger.

This book I dedicate to

Baby Bear … May the seeds planted grow
The Elders … Grandparents raising the young
My Acjachemen Nation … The coastal Southern California Indians

To all that walked on my path in this memorable journey.

# Table of Contents

## Chapter 1

# The Forbidden Gift

It is the end of a beautiful Indian summer, when the leaves are turning shades of reds, yellows, and oranges.

A cool, crisp, bite in the clean mountain air and a thick layer of fog hug the forest floor. As morning approaches the fog lifts, leaving a fine mist that showers beads of liquid diamonds onto the tall old growth trees, the beautiful ferns, berry bushes, and the thick moss that covers much of the forest. A blue jay yells across the quietness like an annoying alarm clock. The bright sun, rising above the mountain tops, sends sharp rays of yellow and white light through the trees, making the diamond mist gleam throughout the forest. Awakening animals lift their heads to see a wonderland of sparkle. The breath of the Creator softly breaths on a beautifully spun spider's web, making it dance softly between two Sgurd Berry bushes, while drops of mist roll slowly along the strands of the intricately woven web.

Suddenly, breaking the silence of the forest is the sound of rustling branches and the rumble of a deep-throated grunt.

The spider's web begins to shake violently as a huge, black paw shoots up between the two Sgurd Berry bushes, ripping a berry from its stem. The strands of the lacy web are stretched to its breaking point and snap, sending the sparkling diamond beads and leaves sailing through the air, as the giant paw descends back into the brush where Yobdab, an immense black bear, loudly gobbles up the huge, juicy berry. After he is finished eating, saliva dripping from his mouth down to his chest, Yobdab rolls over and out from under the bush and tries to stand.

Grabbing the berry bush with his fruit-stained paw, he places his right knee on the ground and pushes his heavy body upward, but he breaks the branch and losing his balance, stumbling forward and crashing through the bush. Yobdab rolls head over heel several times before a giant old growth cedar tree catches his big, boxy head, bringing him to a sudden stop.

The "thump" against the solid tree trunk echoes loud enough to be heard by a small flock of bluebirds flying overhead. They cock their dark blue, pointed heads to the left side, in the direction of the noise, only to see Yobdab, crazy again from

the intoxicating juices of the Sgurd Berry.

Shaking their heads in amazement, they continue their flight as one of them whispers in a disgusted voice, "That boy is never going to learn is he? … Never!"

Rolling over to sit up, moaning and rubbing his bruised head, Yobdab tries again to get up. This time he makes it. Using the cedar tree again, he digs his long bear claws into its trunk and pulls himself up, and then slowly walks his front paws back down toward the ground.

Standing on all fours he sways back and forth. He is intoxicated from eating too many Sgurd Berries. Yobdab lowers his head and takes one long, blurry look through the trees ahead of him, rubs his hurt head, yawns and begins his staggering walk back through the forest. Having no concept of time, but thinking, it must be time to get home.

Lrigdoog and Baby Bear are at the river waiting for Yobdab's return. Yobdab was supposed to be out hunting for some food for his family. Instead, he picked, indulged and got so intoxicated on the "Forbidden Fruit" of the Sgurd Berry bush, that he completely forgot his family and fell asleep with not a worry in the forest.

Lrigdoog's sensitive ears pick up a loud commotion behind her and she runs to protect Baby Bear. Quickly her guard is up, her claws and teeth are showing, not knowing what may be coming through the woods. Thank goodness it is only Yobdab, who clumsily stumbles out of the woods, very happy to see his wife and Baby Bear.

Lrigdoog, after breathing a sigh of relief that she and Baby Bear are not in danger, is not too happy to see him. Although she is relieved to see that he is back and he is all right, she also sees that he has come back empty handed and is acting a little too nice.

Yobdab senses Lrigdoog's distress and begins talking very gently to her. He is quite good at smooth-talking her into almost anything because of the total admiration that she has for him. Just the sound of his gentle voice makes her forget she is upset with him. He tells her that he has something … a gift … and he wants her to have it. A part of her is still upset with him for returning without food, but he tells her again, in a soft whisper, "I have something for you."

She becomes curious as she thinks, Hmm, he has a gift? What could it be? Then Yobdab, ever so gently, moves his big furry body closer to hers and slowly opens his paw. Sitting on his padded, outstretched paw is some type of berry.

Excited at first, she looks closer only to see the berry sparkle. That kind of sparkle only comes from the Forbidden Fruit! "Are you crazy?" Lrigdoog gasps in a low, deep voice, not wanting Baby Bear to hear as she glances over to the river to see if he is watching them.

"What are you doing ? You … have brought me … the Forbidden Fruit?" She can not believe he is doing this. "I can't eat that, and you shouldn't even have it. You should throw it away!

He tries to speak "But … but …" She cuts him off. "What if Baby Bear sees you eating it? You ARE eating it … aren't you?" He lowers his eyes, not able to look at her.

"Baby Bear will think that it is okay to eat that berry, because he sees you eating it. What if he try's it?. Get rid of it right now!" she says in a very low but angry voice. At the same time she is thinking, how could he be gone all day and night, only to return with the Forbidden Fruit!?

"Oooh my Honey bear, it's all right," Yobdab sings in his still gentle voice and than he loudly hiccups twice, right into Lrigdoog's face. His breath hitting her nose with the sweet sent of the Forbidden Fruit, she is disgusted!

"Oooh … excuse me" he giggles and continues talking to her. "I have been munching on this berry, and what they say is not true. It's not bad for you, and when I eat it, it makes me feel so good. I want you to feel this good, won't you try it? " He begs her. "No!" she says. "No, Yobdab. What in the woods is the matter with you? I will not eat that. It is forbidden. You should not be eating it either." In a lower whisper she says, " I can't believe you! What are you thinking? You need to take the berry, and yourself, and get out of here right now!" she says with determination.

Yobdab pleads in return, "But my Lrigdoog, it is not going to hurt you. Don't be afraid. I promise you will like it. I would not give you something that would hurt you. I only want you to feel good." Moving closer to her and in a softer voice, he tells her  … "If you love me Lrigdoog, if you really love me, you will try it."

Lrigdoog turns her head and looks into Yobdab's big brown eyes. She is almost hypnotized by his soft, alluring voice. She loves him so much that she'd do anything for him. She has been with him almost all her bear life, and now as time

moves on they have Baby Bear and are a family.

He sees her spirit start to melt down. Yobdab tempts her again, slowly extending his paw under her nose. She has never been so close to the Forbidden Fruit. It smells like huckleberries and blackberries all in one, so, so good that her mouth begins to salivate.

Leaning very close to her he whispers into her ear, "Please, my beautiful little wife, show me how much you really love me and taste this sweet berry. Do it for me, do it because you love me." Lrigdoog looks at the sparkling berry in the middle of his outstretched paw, and then up into his big, brown, pleading eyes. "You know I love you. There is no love stronger than my love for you." She looks back down at the beautiful, sparkling, plump berry. It's as if the berry has a mind of it's own and is working with Yobdab, sending it's intoxicating scent right up her nose. She sniffs the berry and her nostrils flare open. She blinks her big brown eyes and slowly she places her paw in his and gently takes the fruit, but does not eat it. She only looks at it laying in the center of her paw. Seeing her hesitation, Yobdab quickly prods her again, "Do it for us, join me in this wonderful, relaxed feeling. Show me you love and trust me. You do, don't you?" he says gently.

Lrigdoog softly says, "Yes, I do." she looks back down at the berry and very slowly takes a bite.

Juice shoots out of the plumb berry and splatters Yobdab's nose. Startled, he giggles as his tongue reaches up and washes the delicious juice off the top of his nose.

Looking back at Lrigdoog, he sees her eyes get big as she licks her lips, and a smile stretches across her beautiful bear face. "Ooooo! This … is … delicious!" she sings. "Why have we been told never to eat it?" "Because the people in Skrof pick it, and they want it all to themselves. You know how the humans are!" he tells her. "It is delicious, but you must only eat a little bit of it at first." It will make your head dizzy if you eat too many."

Baby Bear continues to play with the salmon that Lrigdoog caught for him. He unsuccessfully tries to bite the tail of the salmon just as Lrigdoog takes her second bite from the Forbidden Fruit. She savors the succulent fruit, letting the juice drip down over her furry paw onto the front of her beautifully groomed fur. The sweet taste is inviting and makes her want more.

Beginning to feel relaxed and content, Lrigdoog sits next to Yobdab on

**4**

the grassy knoll overlooking the river. Life is good, and she delights in watching her Baby Bear romping in and out of the water with the salmon. Feeling a surge of love toward Yobdab, who has brought her this tasty gift, she snuggles in closer to him.

The song of the birds seems louder, the water sounds crisper, and her head feels lighter as the wind blows softly across her face.

The two bears enjoy watching Baby Bear with his salmon, and Yobdab offers Lrigdoog another berry. She gladly takes it and pops the whole berry into her mouth.

With her focus back on Yobdab, and his gift of the fruit, Lrigdoog begins to forget about Baby Bear. Feeling peaceful and content, she soon dozes off.

Throughout the late afternoon Lrigdoog passes in and out of a light, sleepy haze. She wakes to enjoy another berry or two, and then, feeling lazy again, falls back into her dreamy sleep.

The battle between Baby Bear and the salmon came to an end long ago, while his parents floated in and out of sleep; the feisty fish slips out of Baby Bear's paws and jumps back into the river swimming away. Baby Bear wonders what went wrong, and vows to get a better hold on the fish the next time.

Jumping out of the water, Baby Bear stops and shakes from the tip of his little black nose to his back paws, knocking himself completely off balance. This makes him giggle as he gets back up and wanders over to join Lrigdoog for some of his mother's warm, sweet bear milk. Smacking his lips, he knows that there is always food to be had at his mother's belly, and he snuggles up to her for some dinner. His mother is in such a deep, sound, sleep that when he moves closer to her she gives a snort and grunt. This makes Baby Bear laugh. She's been sleeping before when he wanted some milk, so this has never been a problem for Baby Bear, he just snuggles in closer to her, trying to find her soft, furry belly. But in her haze, Lrigdoog rolls over on her stomach and knocks Baby Bear completely over.

After rolling end over end a couple of times, he gets back up, shakes off the unusual accident, and crawls back to his mother's side, only to discover that she has

**5**

curled up into a tight ball and hidden his source of milk. Baby Bear can't get to it. Frustrated, he pushes on her with his little paws trying many times to roll her over. Walking around and around he tries finding a way to the milk.

A bit bewildered, Baby Bear gets down on his belly and snuggles in close to Lrigdoog's face. With his little bear tongue he starts kissing her, knowing that his kisses always wake her up. But this time it doesn't work, she doesn't even move. Baby Bear notices that her breathing is unusually heavy, and her breath smells of something very different and sweet. Giving his mother a couple more kisses, he is still unsuccessful and finally has to give up.

Curling up next to his mother, Baby Bear can hear the fish jumping in the water and see the stars begin to shimmer in the crisp, clear, evening sky. It is getting dark and he is cold, and can't understand why his family is not in their cozy den and maybe he should go to sleep on his comfortable mossy bed, except, he doesn't want to leave his mother's side. The cold ground chills him to the bone as the dark of night closes in around them.

Distressed, Baby Bear gets as close as he can to his mother, and with tears in his Baby Bear eyes, he tries to ignore the growling in his belly and falls into a restless sleep.

Morning presses hard on Lrigdoog's face. Waking very slowly she knows right away that she does not feel good. She has a headache, her body hurts, and she is stiff from sleeping out in the cold. Baby Bear, seeing that his mother is awake, jumps at the chance to finally eat. But Lrigdoog is impatient with her cub, and she pushes him away. The last thing that she wants is to have Baby Bear suckling at her belly. She feels angry and awful.

Baby Bear tries again to get next to his mother, and again she pushes her cub away. Not understanding this kind of treatment, Baby Bear slowly walks, with his head hung low, over to a cedar tree and sits. Softly crying, with his little face in his paws, he is crushed and does not understands the way his mother is treating him. Lrigdoog, hearing Baby Bear cry, realizes where she is and how mean she has been. Oh, how guilty she feels! She immediately walks over to Baby Bear and tells

him how sorry she is. She cuddles him close and lets him finally drink her milk.

Baby Bear quickly forgets all that has happened and snuggles close to his mother. As she holds her cub tight, the memory of last night slowly comes back to Lrigdoog. Eating the Forbidden Fruit was a bad thing for her and Yobdab to do, but she cannot forget the decadent taste of the enticing fruit. It has stained her taste buds and marked her memory. Suddenly, she remembers … Yobdab told her last night that he had been munching on the fruit. Hmmm … That would explain his strange behavior lately, and why he would be gone for so long during the day, rarely returning with any food for her and Baby Bear. No doubt he has been hanging around close to the town of Skrof where the Forbidden Fruit is plentiful.

Skrof is a small town nestled in a tight, little valley on the south end of the Cipmylo Forest, which is one of the few untouched, old growth forests left on Earth. Tall firs, pines, and cedar trees branch together to form a lacy canopy high above the forest's floor, occasionally allowing beams of sunlight to filter through and dance on one of the many waterfalls cascading off sheer and jagged cliffs. A well-traveled, two-lane road winds its way up and over a mountainside leading to Skrof, the only town in the forest. It takes a weary traveler through beautiful, but very rough terrain. The journey seems never-ending until, all of a sudden, the small town appears out of nowhere.

The unique town of Skrof, dotted with warm and inviting log homes and well-manicured lawns, has a small population of three hundred. But the laughter of children is infrequently heard. Most of the young have left for larger towns and cities in search of better schools and lives that are more exciting. Few ever return.

The livelihood of the town is solely based on the abundance of the Sgurd Berry. The size of a walnut, the Sgurd Berry ripens to a deep burgundy color. Swirling sparkles of hot pink wrap their way from the top of the plump berry around to the bottom. Its everlasting taste is a combination of sweet, juicy, wild blackberries and bittersweet, red huckleberries. The only place on Earth where the precious Sgurd Berry can be found growing is in the region of the Cipmylo Forest.

Rumor has it, that the Sgurd Berry bush is not a plant that is native to the Cipmylo Forest. In fact … rumor has it that it is a plant not even native to Earth … Legend tells that many, many years ago a comet passed so close to Earth that some of the debris became part of our atmosphere. When pieces of the comet melted, one tiny seed from an unknown planet or galaxy, was released and fell to Earth,

**7**

planting itself deep in the rich soil of the Cipmylo Forest. Only one plant grew from this seed. This plant is called the Mother Lode. The simple act of one leaf or one over ripe berry falling to the ground caused thousands of Sgurd Berry bushes to be born. This is how the Mother Lode seeded the whole area of the Cipmylo Forest. Now other plants seed the area by dropping an overripe berry. The Mother Lode is very unique, unlike all of the other Sgurd Berry plants … it can never be destroyed!

When humans discovered the sparkling berry of the Sgurd Bush, they quickly found that it was a medicinal fruit. It cured a very common and highly contagious disease called Edutitta. This is a disease that infects the cells of the human brain. It causes the mind to see things unrealistically and effects the human's whole attitude, and eventually the health of the infected person deteriorates. The Sgurd Berry almost instantly heals damaged brain cells and allows humans to live healthy lives once again, and think with clear minds. However … to the animals of the Cipmylo Forest, the Sgurd Berry is a poison and is known as the Forbidden Fruit. When eaten it makes the animals drunk and causes them to lose control of their minds. Often, these animals will eventually lose their families, and many will even lose their lives.

8

## Chapter 2

# The Protector

Back near the small cave where Yobdab and Lrigdoog live (just a little ways northwest of Skrof), Baby Bear has finished suckling from his mother's furry belly and is in the field playing with his friends, Raccoon and Rabbit. Lrigdoog, still not feeling well, lies back down next to Yobdab who had rolled under a huge sword fern. He slowly wakes up and tells her that he loves her. She tells him that they should not have eaten the Forbidden Fruit; she has a headache and her stomach hurts. "It is not good for us." Yobdab tells her to eat just half of a Forbidden Fruit. "It will make you feel better," he whispers with a thick and heavy tongue and his eyes half closed.

Lrigdoog wants to refuse. She wants to insist that they never partake of the berries again, but she feels so sick. She thinks that if it will make her feel better, she could just eat half and then never eat another of the Forbidden Fruit again. She looks down at the ground where a couple of berries lie. Reluctantly, she slowly scoops one up into her paw and carefully bites into it, certain to only bite off half.

She wants to eat it quickly, because she is never going to touch it again. But the sweet smell goes up her nose and the taste of the berry is sooo good. She slides it back and forth over her tongue before she swallows.

The berry's sweet juice really is like nothing she has ever tasted before, and as she sits there letting herself be taunted by the site of the other half of the berry, she realizes that she is already feeling a little better. The pounding in her head has softened, and the sickness in her stomach has begun to subside. The berry tastes so good, and she feels so much better, that she cannot keep herself from eating the other half of the berry. In fact, that one berry leads to another and then another. She cannot seem to stop; she doesn't want to stop …

That night Baby Bear finds himself in the same situation as the night before. He is made to sleep out in the cold with an empty and very hungry tummy. That day marks the beginning of many difficult days to come for Baby Bear.

Baby Bear learns quickly to fend for himself, as his parents continue to eat the Forbidden Fruit day after day. One day he almost doesn't make it out of the rising water of the creek, and there are several times when he wanders too far from the den and ends up lost. Luckily, there are other animals around who know him and are able to help him get back home.

Talk spreads quickly throughout the forest about Yobdab and Lrigdoog eating the Forbidden Fruit and hanging around with other animals who also indulge. Lrigdoog and Yobdab have always been respected and looked upon as good parents and loving mates. So, when they turn to the Forbidden Fruit and begin to neglect Baby Bear, themselves, and the rest of their usual friends, the animals are in shock. It doesn't take long for the talk to reach the ears of Mama Bear, Baby Bear's grandmother.

Mama Bear lives a full four-day journey away, deep into another part of the Cipmylo Forest called Tserofniar.

Mama Bear has not made the journey to Lrigdoog and Yobdab's home since Baby Bear was two months old. Hearing this bad news about them from the bluebirds, fear wells up in the pit of her soul and a sick feeling enters Mama Bear. Without hesitation, Mama Bear leaves at once. As she embarks on

the four-day journey, her only thoughts are of Baby Bear, his care, and safety.

She must somehow make the journey in three days instead of four. There was a time that she could make this particular trip in two days, if she really needed to, but time is now starting to show on Mama Bear's bones. Her body is not as agile as it used to be. She is learning that the gift of getting older has its price.

Normally, her journey to Skrof would be a pleasant one. Traveling through the Cipmylo Forest is quite an adventure, because the terrain is different throughout. However, there is no time to be wasted on this trip. Mama Bear is on a mission, and all of the animals who see her know it, and know why. The closer to Baby Bear she gets, the more horror stories she hears. When she finally reaches the area where Baby Bear lives, she stays at a distance so that she can watch with her own knowing and experienced eyes. She wants to see what is happening, instead of bursting in on Lrigdoog and Yobdab and accusing them of wrong-doings.

For several days Mama Bear watches and listens, and to her disappointment the stories she has heard are true. Baby Bear's parents are, indeed, partaking of the Forbidden Fruit. They don't even realize that they are being watched, that is how vulnerable and unsafe they are. Mama Bear is devastated and angry. Her innocent baby grandchild has to fend for himself. He is hungry, dirty, and in harm's way. She is furious!

For the next few days Mama Bear stays close to Baby Bear but stays hidden. She even secretly helps him out when he has a close call at the river, because it has become a raging force due to the heavy rains that are now upon them. Then, on the fourth day, Mama Bear hears the all-too-familiar sounds of danger approaching. The hackle in the middle of her back goes up, fear shooting like ice water through every cell of her being, and she moves as fast as she can toward Baby Bear. She fears that she might not reach him in time.

From a distance hunters have spotted Lrigdoog and Yobdab sleeping under a Sgurd Berry bush, and they move closer with their guns raised and ready to fire. Lrigdoog and Yobdab hear sticks breaking and finally become aware of the approaching hunters. They have both eaten so many berries, that they are disoriented and it is a terrible struggle to wake themselves up. "Baby Bear?" Lrigdoog calls frantically, but she does not know where to look for him.

The hunters' sounds crash closer and closer. Lrigdoog and Yobdab run as fast as their wobbly legs will carry them into the forest, away from the hunters, while

**11**

looking for Baby Bear at the same time.

Baby Bear is on the other side of the creek looking for food. He has a strange, sick feeling in the pit of his stomach. Something he has never felt before. His keen ears hear unfamiliar sounds; voices, unlike animals, and sticks breaking. He has never felt this scared, nor has he ever been told about hunters.

Hearing the thrashing noises nearly upon him, he instinctively knows that he must run away as fast as his little paws will carry him. As the trees close in around him, he doesn't know which way to go as he desperately searches for his mother and father. Suddenly, he comes to a complete stop. Eyes wide open, and filled with fear, Baby Bear's paws are frozen to the ground beneath him.

"There he is!" one of the hunters yells and immediately starts shooting his gun at Baby Bear. The sound is deafening. A bullet flies past Baby Bear striking a tree, splitting part of its trunk open. He flinches away from the tree. "Zing! Zing!" Two more bullets race past Baby Bear's head, and another hunter yells wildly, "I got 'em, I got 'em!"

Baby Bear lifts his paws and runs blindly past a giant old cedar tree when Mama Bear runs out in front of him. "Come with me, Baby Bear!" she yells. "Hurry! Hurry! Come with me and run as fast as you can. Run, Baby Bear, run. Run for your life!"

They run for a good mile through thick brush and swamp land. They run into the part of the forest that grows behind the town of Skrof, where Mama Bear knows that the terrain is too treacherous for most hunters to walk, let alone run. This is why they have gone this way, and as she runs Mama Bear thinks about Lrigdoog and Yobdab, did they make it? Could they have pulled themselves out of their stupor to run fast enough to be safe? She doubts it, and tears of grief well up in her heart. She keeps going to save Baby Bear and herself, for she knows now, that she will be the only one able to take care of him.

Usually, Baby Bear would have a difficult time keeping up with Mama Bear, but a newly felt emotion … FEAR! … is driving Baby Bear like never before. He is right on Mama Bear's heels. The faster they run, the more distant the sounds of the hunters become.

Finally, when there are no more fearful sounds to be heard, and Mama Bear feels that it is safe to stop, she turns and grabs a hold of Baby Bear and hugs him tightly in her protective, loving arms. Baby Bear is sobbing and grabbing onto Mama Bear. "It's okay, my little Baby Bear. We are safe now. You are going to be

**12**

just fine. Mama Bear is here now to protect you, and I am going to take you on a journey to a place where you will be safe," she says in a soothing voice. Baby Bear is crying and shaking so badly that he cannot talk or let go of Mama Bear. She holds him close to her and tells him that it is okay to cry and to know his fear. "Remember this feeling," she says, "and remember what fear is, Baby Bear, because it will teach you as you grow."

After awhile Baby Bear calms down, and he looks up at Mama Bear with his eyes still filled with tears and his breath short, "Oh, Mama Bear, I was so scared. Who were they and what were those loud noises? How did you find me? Where are my parents?"

"They were hunters with guns," Mama Bear tells him. "I will explain more later, but know, Baby Bear, that I have been watching you, and I will always watch over you." "Thank you, Mama Bear. I love you," Baby Bear whispers while looking into Mama Bear's huge, loving, eyes. "I love you too, my little Baby Bear," she says, as she dries his eyes and kisses him. "But we must keep moving. We have quite a journey ahead of us." She puts him down and moves quickly, not giving Baby Bear a chance to ask another question.

Through the Cipmylo Forest, Mama Bear and Baby Bear travel. Baby Bear has never seen this part of the forest and he likes it. Soon, they both hear waters dancing, and Mama Bear says to Baby Bear, "Let's stop and drink the juice of the earth." Making their way down a hill toward the babbling sounds, they find a nice creek with waters racing off of tiered, flat rocks, splashing from one rock to another. Beautiful sword ferns and ivy gently lace the banks of the creek.

"Oh, yes, Mama Bear, I am thirsty," says Baby Bear, while jumping into the middle of the creek's bed. After

he drinks the cool, clean water and plays for just a minute, he gets out, shakes, and walks over to a bush and sniffs the deep burgundy berry dangling in front of him, bringing back a very familiar smell. He reaches his furry little paw up toward the bush and picks a big, fat, juicy berry.

Baby Bear has his eyes closed and his mouth wide open, with the berry half way in, when the swift and firm paw of Mama Bear swipes the berry out of his mouth. This startles Baby Bear so badly that he lets out a short scream and begins to cry. Mama Bear takes him into her loving arms to calm him and tells him, "Baby Bear, please don't cry. Mama Bear is so sorry that she scared you, but you were about to eat a kind of berry that is very bad for you, so bad that it is called the Forbidden Fruit by all of the animals in the forest." Baby Bear, wiping his tears and taking a short breath, replies, "But I am hungry, Mama Bear, and my mother and father eat this kind of berry when they are hungry. I watched them." Baby Bear puts his head down and sucks on one of his little claws as he looks at the ground.

"Yes, Baby Bear, I watched them too, but they were not supposed to be eating these kinds of berries. If you eat the Forbidden Fruit, they will make you no longer care, and will make you forget about what is important in life. You must keep your mind and your spirit and your body clean and clear at all times if you are to survive and make a good life for yourself."

Raising her voice a notch, she continues, "Please, Baby Bear, look into my eyes when I talk to you. Remember to look into the eyes of any animal who talks to you, and any animal who you talk to and you will know how sincere that animal is. They will also know how sincere you are.

"Look in my eyes as I say these words to you Baby Bear. Remember, and promise me, that you will NOT eat the Forbidden Fruit. It is not for you; it is only for the humans to eat. For them it is medicine, but for animals it is danger. Please, promise me, Baby Bear!"

Baby Bear, looking into Mama Bear's eyes sees instantly her sincerity as she speaks these words. He can see, and even feel, her emotions just by looking into her eyes. He nods his head, still taking in all that he has heard and all that has happened in just one day, and answers her, "Yes, Mama Bear, I promise never to eat the Forbidden Fruit. I promise."

After Mama Bear gives Baby Bear another hug and kiss, she takes him over to a bush that is flourishing with plump, juicy blueberries. "Eat this berry," she says

to Baby Bear. "It is good." It takes Mama Bear and Baby Bear four days to reach Tserofniar, the most magical and beautiful part of the Cipmylo Forest. Here more rain falls than in the area of Skrof, so the terrain is greener than in any other part of the forest. Giant trees grow in mystical shapes with stocky trunks that look like the Creator twirled and twisted them out of a bed of lush greenery. Dripping with moss, their limbs branch out as if they are raising them to the sky, giving thanks to the Creator. Moss grows so thick that Baby Bear's paw's sink into the ground with each step he takes, making him feel as if he is walking on fluffy clouds. Even the bird's beautiful songs sound different here in this part of the forest. It is as if they sing in orchestration with one another, while melting harmonies rise and fall from nearly every tree.

It is early morning, and Mama Bear and Baby Bear have been traveling all night. As Baby Bear hears the babbling of water, he catches the concentrated, sweet smell of huckleberries drifting on the breeze, and his little belly gurgles with the morning sounds of hunger. As they pass through some thick brush, Mama Bear suddenly stops and stands up. Baby Bear is following so close to her that he bumps into her right hip. Starting to bounce off he grabs a hold of her leg to keep from falling. Mama Bear looking down at him, chuckles to herself. He looks up at her and wonders why they have stopped so abruptly. Mama Bear is tall and strong, and Baby Bear feels safe and protected next to her. So as he sees her looking ahead, he cautiously peeks around her in the same direction to see what she looking at.

Baby Bear lets go a soft gasp, and his little mouth opens in amazement as he sings … "Ohhh, Mama Bear!" He lets go of her leg and scurries in front of her and stands up as tall as he can on his little hind legs. Never has Baby Bear seen anything more beautiful!

A lake, with water so still that it looks like a mirror, stretches out before them. The reflection of the morning light dances across the glassy surface to the other side where a waterfall drops into three tiers and spills into the lake at the far end. Wild crabapple trees and many different types of berry bushes surround the lake.

A pang of joy wells up in Mama Bear's heart to see Baby Bear's reaction and to see him so happy. She lowers herself back down onto all four paws, kisses Baby Bear, and nudges him with her big, wet nose. "Come, Baby Bear," she says with a twinkle in her eye, "this is your new home. Let's go see."

"This is where I am going to live from now on, Mama Bear? Why?" Baby Bear

looks into her eyes and asks.

Mama Bear tells him, "Your parents know where I live, and if they are all right, they will know where to come. Trust me, Baby Bear, everything will be fine, and you will be happy here."

Baby Bear does trust Mama Bear, and without asking anything more, he runs ahead of her on the path that she has created leading to her cave. Mama Bear's cave is on the side of the mountain not far from the waterfall, and it is an easy climb. When they reach the entrance Baby Bear stops, turns around, and stands up to look at the lake from this new view.

Intuitively, he knows that he must begin to familiarize himself with the area right away. Mama Bear watches him and knows what he is doing. This brings her comfort, because he is using his intuition.

Entering Mama Bear's cave is a delight. It is clean and smells of fresh cedar and pine. Her bed is king-sized and overstuffed with layers of cedar boughs and soft oak leaves nestled under a thick blanket of fluffy, curly moss. Mama Bear lets Baby Bear have a good look at his new home and then remembers hearing his little tummy growling with hunger when they first came upon the lake. "Let's go eat," she says to Baby Bear, "and then we will make your bed right next to mine." He is so happy with that and heads out of the cave to search for food.

After filling his belly with all of the huckleberries he could possibly eat, Baby Bear starts gathering moss, leaves, and boughs for his new bed. He wants a bed just like Mama Bear's bed, and he wants it to be as close to her as possible.

That night, Mama Bear catches dinner for them out of the lake. After eating a good meal of salmon and more huckleberries, they both go into the lake to bathe. Mama Bear tells Baby Bear how important it is to be clean every night before going to bed. "A good bear is a clean bear!" she says as she laughs and splashes water at him.

After they shake the water out of their fur and dry, Mama Bear and Baby Bear walk back to the cave and climb into their cozy, mossy beds. Settling down to sleep, Mama Bear says to Baby Bear, "Now put your back right up against mine and snuggle as close as you can."

Before he closes his eyes, Mama Bear says, "Wanna race?" Curious, Baby Bear, asks, "What kind of race?". "Well, a sleep race, of course! You mean you have never had a sleep race before?" she says. "No …" he answers, scrunching up little nose. "I will say, 'On your mark,' and you will say, 'Get set,' and then we will both say 'SLEEP!'

at the same time. Whoever goes to sleep first, wins!"

"Oh, Mama Bear, you're so funny. Is that really the race?"

"Yes, you ready to play?"

"OK" Baby Bear says with excitement in his voice.

"On your mark . . ." Mama Bear starts.

"Get set . . ." Baby Bear adds.

"Sleep!" they both say together, and a hushed silence fills the cave. Baby Bear breathes a deep sigh of relief, feeling safe and loved again, then closes his eyes and falls into a deep, relaxing sleep.

Mama Bear can feel Baby Bear's little body slowly go limp as his breathing calms and he relaxes into a soft sleep. Mama Bear feels the emotions welling up inside her and tears fill her eyes. She loves Baby Bear and is relieved he is with her.

She lies there for a while thinking about the chain of events over these past days. She wonders about Lrigdoog and Yobdab and tries to sense if they are still alive. She also wonders about Baby Bear and how he is going to adapt to this new lifestyle with his Mama Bear and without his parents.

This is certainly not something she had expected. Mama Bear had already raised a cub of her own, Lrigdoog, Baby Bear's mother, and now she is enjoying the comforts of Tserofniar. It is an area of the forest that Mama Bear put a great deal of time and love into developing. She rid the area of all the Forbidden Fruit that used to grow there in abundance. All of the bushes except one.

For many years now there has been one bush of the Forbidden Fruit growing in the Cipmylo Forest. It is located just outside of her den, right next to the giant old growth cedar tree. It is called the Mother Lode of all the Sgurd Berry bushes. This is something that Mama Bear has been trying to keep secret.

She tells all of the other animals that the plant is allowed to stay there, so that she can use it to teach all of the baby animals of Tserofniar what it looks like. This is so that when they grow up, they will know not to touch it or eat it. Only Mama Bear knows that there is much more to the story than that.

# Chapter 3
# Counting the Stars

It doesn't take Baby Bear long to adapt to his new surroundings and to his new, comfortable lifestyle. Throughout the next couple of years Mama Bear teaches him how to fish, what berries are good to eat, and what berries are bad to eat. She teaches him how to live by the changing of the seasons and he learns to recognize the shifting of the full moon to the new and to watch the color of the leaves turn from many different shades of green to bright yellows, oranges, and reds. In her soft spoken words she tells him that when the leaves fall, they die in one way, but then in another way they live, because they provide nutrients for new plants that will come up in place of the leaves that fall. She also explains to him why his beautiful thick fur coat loses much of its fur and grows thinner just before the long, hot days of summer come to the forest.

Mama Bear teaches Baby Bear to pay careful attention to the hardest working little animals in the forest, the ants. When the ants are working especially hard, it will be a sign for Baby Bear to expect a long, hard, winter. This will mean that they will need to be well prepared, just like the ants and the other animals of the forest, during this time of quiet solitude and reflection.

Most importantly, Mama Bear tells Baby Bear why she patrols Tserofniar daily, looking for any Forbidden Fruit that may accidentally sprout up. She has seen to it that the only Forbidden Fruit bush to grow in Tserofniar is the Mother Lode that grows where she can keep a watchful eye on it and use it to teach the other animals of its dangers. She tells Baby Bear, "As long as the Forbidden Fruit does not grow in the region of Tserofniar, there will be no reason for humans to venture into this part of the forest. And if there is no Forbidden Fruit growing here, the animals will not be so tempted to eat it. This is why we must patrol Tserofniar nearly every day, to look for the Forbidden Fruit and anything else that should not be here." Baby Bear looks right into Mama Bear's eyes, as she has taught him, while she explains this to him. He can see her sincerity and trusts immediately that this will be a very important thing for them to do together while he is growing up with Mama Bear in Tserofniar.

On a beautiful Indian summer's evening, Mama Bear sits down to relax at the edge of the mountain where she takes in the view of the whole valley of Tserofniar below. As she rests her back against the trunk of an old alder tree, and looks out over the land, she remembers all of the good times she has had in her life here in this part of the Cipmylo Forest. The sun casts reds, pinks, gray-blues, purples and a touch of yellow across the darkening sky. Stars twinkle on the horizon and Baby Bear walks over and lays his furry body next to Mama Bear, placing his little boxy head against her right shoulder. Baby Bear breathes out a whispered sigh of relief. It always feels good to relax next to Mama Bear, she is his comfort zone.

Mama Bear softly says, "Isn't this beautiful?" Baby Bear agrees and says, "Oh yes, look at the stars Mama Bear. Do you think anybody lives out there?"

"Oh, yes … somebody lives out there. They may not look like you and me … they may look like giant flowers that are all different colors and talk a different language … but somebody lives there." As she says this Baby Bear watches as Mama Bear lifts her left paw into the air and waves it at the moon and stars. He laughs and asks her what she is doing. "I'm saying, 'Hi!' You never know if someone is watching, and I want them to know that I am friendly. Wave, Baby Bear, and say, 'Hi!" Baby Bear lifts his right paw into the air and starts waving and yelling, "Hi! Hello! My name is Baby Bear. Hi!"

Both he and Mama Bear start laughing together, and Mama Bear hugs him tight. "I love you, Baby Bear," she says, with the warmth of laughter in her voice. "I love you too," he answers. She tells him "For the rest of your forever, don't forget to count the stars at night, to wave to the moon, and to throw a thought towards the sun. They will wave back, Baby Bear. Know that you are never alone … you are never alone!"

Baby Bear has grown up with a small group of friends in Tserofniar. Not long after arriving he met Flagtail. Flagtail was a young buck back then, who was the same age as Baby Bear. Flagtail's parents brought him to this part of the forest when he was a baby and left him to be taken care of by Mama Bear. They had been eating the Forbidden Fruit and could not take care of him; they knew that she would. Now, Flagtail is a massive, healthy, male deer thanks to the care of Mama Bear.

Buttercup is an inquisitive and smart little black bear who grew up not too far from where Baby Bear lived. Buttercup adores Baby Bear and loves to follow him around. She is a year younger than Baby Bear and lives with her mother. Buttercup

does not know where her father is, and like Baby Bear and Flagtail's parents, he also began to eat the Forbidden Fruit and became crazy on it. All she knows is that he was last seen in the forest somewhere near Skrof.

Then there is Wapiti. He is a stately elk who is just a little bit older than Baby Bear. Wapiti is also an orphan because of the intoxicating Forbidden Fruit. Mama Bear raised him along with Baby Bear and Flagtail. Of the three, Wapiti has become Baby Bear's best friend because they grew up so close together.

The four of them are great friends and constant companions. Buttercup is the youngest among them, with an innocent but funny personality. The three boys all watch over her and protect her. Although the four of them are the best of friends, there are also other critters that live in the surrounding area who are also their friends: Beaver Boy; Gruff, the cottontail rabbit; Color, the skunk; and of course,

the squirrels, rodents, and birds. They all watch out for one another, learn to fish together, play together, and often lie beneath the wild crabapple tree in the open field and talk … One day, while lying beneath the crabapple tree, Beaver Boy asks Baby Bear, "Where is your mother and father?"

A far away look fills Baby Bear's eyes as he thinks about how little he remembers about Lrigdoog and Yobdab. He remembers them eating the forbidden fruit, though, and the day the hunters came. Instantly, he can hear in his head the loud blasts of gunshots, again he feels the fear that grew inside him that day, and recalls the pounding of his little paws as they hit the ground, in panic, following Mama Bear away … away.

"I don't know," he says simply. "They eat the Forbidden Fruit and are different."

"Oh," says Buttercup, nodding her head, "I know what you mean. My dad eats the Forbidden Fruit too. One day he got into a huge argument with my mom, and she told him to leave the cave and don't come back until he has stopped eating the Forbidden Fruit. I sure do miss him and wish that he would stop eating that awful berry. I am never going to eat that berry! Never!"

"Na, me neither," says Baby Bear.

"Neither am I," whispers Flagtail.

"Not me!" everyone agrees, this is bad fruit and it does  bad things.

Mama Bear has been the protector of this part of the forest, keeping unwanted animals that partake of the Forbidden Fruit out of it and destroying any bushes that might crop up. She will continue to do this until Baby Bear is full grown and takes over her role as protector. Mama Bear has watched Baby Bear's round little body grow into a robust, healthy, boar of a bear over the past several years. She is well aware that his strength and character have become well known in the region of Tserofniar. Already he is creative, swift, and knows how to use his intuition. He is growing into a grand warrior of all warriors, and his strength is not to be reckoned with, even at this early age.

# The Capture

On the other side of the Cipmylo Forest, near Skrof, Baby Bear's mother and father, Lrigdoog and Yobdab live in memory of the hunters on that painful day. Not knowing that Mama Bear saved Baby Bear. They are now living with a band of animals that are also eating the Forbidden Fruit. They have been terrorizing the town of Skrof, and the people of the town fear for their lives and their economy.

There are so many animals now eating the Sgurd Berries that many of the bushes, which were once so plentiful in and around Skrof, are becoming barren, producing less and less fruit. The town depends on the harvesting of the berries, used to cure the disease Edutitta, as its main source of income. They process and ship the berry all around the world, this being the only place where the Sgurd Berry is known to grow.

The people of Skrof live in more and more fear of losing their lives, because many of the animals become crazed when they eat the Sgurd Berry. Creatures, who are normally gentle and would never harm a human being, are often violent, filled with a sense of false power that makes them believe that they are invincible. This is happening more and more as the Sgurd Berries become scarce, because the animals keep eating them in order to keep from being sick, and because they love the feeling of being intoxicated.

Yobdab and two of his friends, Elbuort and Regnad, are three of the animals that have become the most crazed from the juices of the Forbidden Fruit, and they are the most daring as the supply of berries dwindles. One day, they start talking amongst themselves …

Elbuort, a big brown bear, with bald patches all over his body and bad breath (from overindulging in the Forbidden Fruit) says, in his raspy voice to

Regnad and Yobdab, "Let's go to Skrof. I know that they have a big building filled with the Forbidden Fruit. The people there pick 'em and put 'em in there. We can go in and eat 'em all up! After all, they are from OUR forest anyway!" Regnad, who is a lazy, middle-sized, black bear, looks at Yobdab with a big mischievous grin plastered across his face. Yobdab smiles back at him as they both say, "Yeah, let's go!"

That same afternoon a storm rolls over the mountain, settling in the valley of Skrof. The people of the town hunker down in their homes and wait for the storm to pass. Strong winds whip through a good part of the Cipmylo Forest, but it does not stop the three renegades as they head for the town. The wind and rain, beating down from all directions, make it impossible for the people of Skrof to hear the three power-crazed bears break into the Sgurd Berry factory. Ripping and tearing off one of the two huge wooden doors, Yobdab and his friends enter the old, cedar-shake building. Once inside, their eyes grow as big as oranges and their mouths drop wide open as the overhead lights reveal the contents of the building. They are stunned at what they see … rows and rows of tall wooden barrels filled with the Forbidden Fruit!

They slowly look at each other, and Elbuort lets out a short, deep grunt; nothing more need be said. All three of them head toward the barrels and begin their eating frenzy. Regnad stands on his back paws, placing his front paws on either side of one of the barrels, and shoves his face deep into the middle of the barrel, filling his wide opened mouth with berries. Yobdab and Elbuort do the same.

The more berries they eat, the clumsier they become, knocking over barrels and tables, laughing wildly at each other all the while. Elbuort begins throwing berries at the other two, starting a berry fight, and in a short time the place is a disaster. Finally, covered with berry juice, slobbering all over themselves, and wallowing on the now filthy floor, one by one they eventually pass into a deep, drunken sleep.

Morning soon comes, and the storm passes, calming down to a mild rain. The three renegades lie fast asleep in their own mess of mass destruction, completely oblivious to the workers arriving for the first morning shift at the factory. The workers cannot believe the site of the mess or of the three bears passed out among the half-empty, knocked over, barrels. The bears do not wake up; they are too drunk. The people do not know what to do and start whispering to one another, careful not to wake the drunken bears. Somebody says, "Let's kill them." "Yes," somebody else agrees, "go get the guns. Hurry!"

But before they are able to leave, Sam, who has lived in Skrof all of his life, steps forward and yells, "No! Let's capture them and put them in my cellar. We can help them to stop eating the Sgurd Berries. I'm sure they are good bears. Their minds are altered now, and they don't understand the consequences of their actions. If we help them, maybe we can save our town."

As the people look at the drunken bears sprawled across the floor, some disagree, and others begin to mumble in agreement. A angry woman steps forward and asks, "How will helping these disgusting bears save our town?"

Finally, one man says, "Maybe he is right. If we help these bears to get well, maybe they will go back into the forest and help the other animals stop eating the Sgurd Berries. If the animals stop eating the berries, there will be plenty for us to continue harvesting." Thinking about this for a moment, many begin to nod their heads, finally understanding. They all agree and several leave to go and gather ropes and blankets instead of guns.

The first time that they try to move the unconscious bears, after tying them up and sliding the blankets underneath them, the bears are just way too heavy, and … WHEW! … they smell so bad! But something has to be done quickly before they come out of their stupor. Finally, with the help of a forklift, they load the bears into the back of a truck, that is normally used to haul berries, and drive them over to Sam's cellar.

The cellar was once used as a root cellar. It is built next to the house and has a ramp at the entrance. The ramp makes it easier to move the bears into the cellar, and the women and children go to gather dry straw, buckets of water, fresh fruit, and healthy vegetables, while the men move the bears from the truck. Then they place everything in the cellar, trying to make it as comfortable for the bears as possible.

It is many hours before Yobdab starts to even move. All three bears are piled next to each other, so when Yobdab moves, he stirs Elbuort and Regnad. They moan as they slowly wake up, their bodies hurting, and all three have terrible headaches. Yobdab is the first to attempt to get up, rolling over very slowly on his side. He lies still for another moment, his eyes still closed, and then gently rolls onto his upset belly. Groaning with each movement he carefully brings his back paws under him and raises his skinny, ragged butt up into the air. He moans and grunts as he raises the front part of his body up next, finally, he is on all fours. Standing straight up, reaching both paws high into the air, he stretches. Than brings his paws down to his belly and scratches, yawning loudly.

After rubbing his eyes, he opens them, and Yobdab cannot believe what he sees! He closes his eyes, rubs them again, and shakes his head before opening them a second time. His mouth drops, and his eyes are as big as saucers, as a screaming, deep growl emerges from Yobdab's mouth. His growl is so loud that it brings Elbuort and Regnad staggering to their feet, and all three bears stand there flabbergasted. "Where are we?" "How did we get here?" "Let's get out of here!"

Running on all fours, they look frantically for a way out. But there is none. The windows are too high, and the big double doors are locked tight. As they continue to run and search, they try digging, but the ground is solid, like rock. The bears can see people looking at them through the windows above.

One of the men yells down to them, "You broke into our Sgurd Berry factory last night and did a lot of damage. You ate up and destroyed most of the berries that we had stored and became so stupid that you passed out on the factory floor. We have brought you here to give you a chance. We've given you fresh water, fresh fruits and vegetables, and made you clean, fluffy beds to sleep on. We want to help you rid yourself of the Sgurd Berry. All you are doing is killing yourselves, and we don't want crazy animals like you running around in the forest, eating up all of the Sgurd Berries, and coming into our town like you three did last night. Luckily no one was hurt. Here you will stay until you can leave without needing to eat the Sgurd Berries anymore."

One of the other men looked at the man who was talking and asked, "Do you think they understood what you said?" He shrugs his shoulders and answers, "I don't know, but I know that what we are doing is best for them and us. Let's hope this works" Yobdab stands up on his hind legs, raising his front paws into the air and from the pit of his stomach comes forth a yell that shakes the air around him, "NOOO!!! … " but it comes out sounding like a ferocious growl, scaring all of the people standing around the building. As the thought of Lrigdoog goes through his head, he cries out loud, "She will not know where I am. How will she survive without me? I have to get out of here! Now!" Pacing back and forth, again looking for a way out, he mumbles, "Why did I come into town? All for the love of the Forbidden Fruit! How stupid I am …" He finishes by screaming, "HOW STUPID!"

But there is no way out. The people are taking no chances. The doors are locked tight, and nobody ever opens them; all of their food is lowered through the windows, water runs constantly through a hose and into a watering trough, and they have a small, caged-in yard outside that they can go into, the floors are all cement. They are here to stay. Being confined to the cellar gives Yobdab time to think. What a mess he has created with his life. He has lost his beautiful wife, Lrigdoog, and his only son, Baby Bear, is dead. All because I choose to eat the forbidden fruit. How could I have been so

stupid? He thinks. I miss my Lrigdoog and Baby Bear. I wonder if she is alive and okay? If I ever get out of here, I am going to find her and help her to rid herself of the Forbidden Fruit. Maybe we can start a new life in another part of the forest where it does not grow. "I am so sorry for everything I have done, I am so sorry." He whispers to himself.

28

## Chapter 5

# The Wrath of Mama Bear

Back in the forest Lrigdoog wakes early, lifting up her head so slightly to look around. The fog is thick as it hugs the forest floor, and she is covered with beads of misty water. Over head she hears the distant call of a blue bird. She ate too much of the Forbidden Fruit last night and fell asleep down by the river again instead of sleeping in her cave. She quickly realizes that Yobdab is not there, and she begins to worry. She is upset, because he comes home less and less these days, but she is also very sick to her stomach and needs some more of the Forbidden Fruit to make her feel better. So, she gets up and gently shakes the water from her fur. This adds to the headache that she has, and she complains out loud, while rubbing her wet head, "Ohhh … I don't feel good."

Now, she has to search longer to find any berries, as they are becoming fewer in this area. Between the humans and the animals living here, they are disappearing fast. Finally, she finds a bush with several of the forbidden berries on it. Sitting under the berry bush she begins to eat, and as she munches on her second berry, Lrigdoog can hear the bluebirds flying over. She hears them talking.

"Baby Bear has grown into quite the bear," sings one bird.

"Yes," says another bird, "he has. Mama Bear sure does love that little bear. He is a good bear. Did you see that fish he caught yesterday? It was huge!"

Lrigdoog can't believe her ears! The berry she is eating falls out of her paw, hitting her belly and bouncing onto the ground, rolling past her paw. She thought that Baby Bear had been shot and killed by the hunters that came that awful day so long ago. She whispers to herself, "He was not killed? He is alive? Oh my Creator … We couldn't find him when we went back after the hunters left. I thought they had taken him away."

She has been trying to drown her guilt and sorrow for almost three years, because she had eaten so much of the Forbidden Fruit that day that she could not help Baby Bear when the hunters came. Tears well up in her bloodshot eyes and drop to the ground, as she slowly forces herself to stand. Chills well up from inside her body and in almost a state of panic she says, "I must go see for myself if Baby

Bear is really alive."

Mama Bear lives far away, but Lrigdoog must go. She wishes Yobdab were here to go with her, but the thought of Baby Bear … alive! …makes her want to leave right away. Lrigdoog leaves for Tserofniar, but not before grabbing the last of the Forbidden Fruit on the bush, and the one that she dropped on the ground next to her.

It should have only taken Lrigdoog four days to make the journey to Tserofniar. It takes her eight full days. She partakes of the Forbidden Fruit all the way there until she reaches Mama Bear's part of the Cipmylo Forest where no Forbidden Fruit bushes are allowed to grow.

Stepping into Tserofniar is like stepping into another world for Lrigdoog. She crosses a small creek that divides the regions, and immediately her paws sink into a thick carpet of moss as she steps out of the cool water onto the other side. The trees are dripping with flowers, fruit, and curly, soft green, moss. It has been so long since she has been here that she has forgotten how beautiful it is. Everything is so green. But … there is no Forbidden Fruit, Mama Bear has made certain of that … and Lrigdoog wants some so badly right now. To find any, though, she will have to travel back out of Tserofniar, but she must see Baby Bear first.

Trying to remembering her way, Lrigdoog heads for Mama Bear's den. It takes her half of a day to get there; she had forgotten how far it was from the border through Tserofniar. The trees and berry bushes have grown so much since the last time she was here. She keeps saying over and over "how beautiful it is." When she finally gets close to Mama Bears cave, she tries to stay at a distance and not be seen, so she hides behind a thick sword fern. It doesn't work. Mama Bear is too alert and too aware of the happenings around her and Baby Bear. There is no greater wrath than that of Mama Bear when it comes to Baby Bear.

Mama Bear is shocked to see that Lrigdoog is alive, but also can smell the sweet scent of the Forbidden Fruit that permeates Lrigdoog's body. Mama Bear immediately circles around the forest and easily sneaks up behind Lrigdoog, surprising her. "What are you doing here, Lrigdoog?" Mama Bear demands in a low, angry voice.

Lrigdoog is so startled and scared that she jumps back and trips over a log, flying backwards into a blueberry bush, sending berry's flying into the air. Lying on her back, moaning, and stunned, she looks up to see Mama Bear standing over her with her paws on her hips, the sun light bouncing off Mama Bears back. Lrigdoog can barely see the frown on her face. "Ah … ah … hello, Mama Bear. I … I heard that Baby Bear is alive, and I want to see him," she demands as she gains her composure, standing on all four paws and shaking her head.

Mama Bear looks Lrigdoog up one end and down the other and raises her eyebrow with a scornful look. "Lrigdoog, you are Baby Bear's mother; that cannot be taken away from you. But … I will not allow Baby Bear the torture of seeing his mother, for the first time in three years, looking like you do! You look awful! You smell and your fur is matted, dirty, and stained with the juices of the Forbidden Fruit. I could smell you before I saw you. You reek of the intoxicating scent of the Forbidden Fruit." Mama Bear shakes her head in disgust as she continues. " And do you expect him to look into your bloodshot eyes and see love in his long lost mother? I think not.

No! I, will not have this for him. If you really want to see Baby Bear, you go and clean yourself up. You stop eating the Forbidden Fruit and get your mind, body, and spirit back. Then, and not until then, are you allowed." With even a deeper voice and whisper, Mama Bear leans towards her and adds, "Do you understand?"

With tears in her eyes Lrigdoog, looks at Mama Bear, choked up with the stabbing words that she has said to her. Nodding her head, she whispers, "Yes, I understand." She then lowers her head, dropping huge tears to the ground, and slowly walks away, still looking for a glimpse of Baby Bear as she goes.

Mama Bear's heart and spirit ache for Lrigdoog, but she stands firm. Lrigdoog is where she is because

she wants to be there. She choose to eat the forbidden fruit and live the life she is living. Mama Bear knows that Lrigdoog can also choose a life free from the forbidden fruit. Mama Bear loves Baby Bear with every ounce of her being and will protect him with her last breath on this beautiful earth; she will protect him from the spirit side of life also.

Watching Lrigdoog walk away, Mama Bear thinks how sad life is turning. More and more animals of the forest are partaking of the Forbidden Fruit and losing their way. They are losing their families and the young animals are starting to follow their example. Mama Bear is determined to stop this. She has to be the wall between Baby Bear the Forbidden Fruit and it's repercussions.

Mama Bear returns to the open field where Baby Bear is relaxing with his friends. Although she saw Lrigdoog turn and walk away, she remains on high alert knowing that Lrigdoog could still be in the area and may not have the sense to leave. But Lrigdoog listens to Mama Bear, and instead of heading back to her old home, she crosses Tserofniar and takes the opposite path out of Mama Bear's part of the forest. She is heading toward Noitalosi, a region located on the highest mountain range of the Cipmylo Forest. She must get clean and she remembers hearing that Noitalosi is a place of great healing. This is where she must go, not home to Yobdab or the Forbidden Fruit but to a new and clean life. She wants to be with Baby Bear.

The terrain to Noitalosi is so rugged that no humans have ever explored it, and few animals dare to venture to the top. It is an ancient volcano that has been inactive for hundreds of years. It will take Lrigdoog eight days of slowly working and zigzagging her way up the mountain, but she knows that this is the only place that she can go in order to clean herself up.

With each step her body gets sicker. Not eating the Forbidden Fruit in days makes her body ache and her head hurt terribly. She breaks out in cold sweats and is short of breath, but she does not stop, she is determined to straighten out her life and rid herself of the Forbidden Fruit. She loves Baby Bear so much that she will do

whatever it takes to make life right again.

      While she climbs, Lrigdoog does a lot of thinking. Mama Bear was right. How could I have shown my love to Baby Bear through my bloodshot eyes? How could I hold him next to me, smelling so badly and with such dirty fur? How could he see love in my broken, lifeless spirit? What was I thinking? That was just it, she knows now that she wasn't thinking clearly and had not been ever since the day that Yobdab handed her the gift of the sweet tasting Forbidden Fruit and she so willingly excepted it.

      Climbing upward, she struggles with the meanest mountain of them all. The taste of Forbidden Fruit is ingrained throughout her whole body, and every muscle and every nerve keeps screaming for more. Everything she eats along the way reminds her even more of the taste of the Forbidden Fruit, but she stays strong and refuses to go back. Knowing if she did, she would not return. She must keep going up.

      She wants her Baby Bear back and to have a normal life again, like the life that she had before the Forbidden Fruit, but she knows that it will never be the same. She knows that her Yobdab has gone too far with the Forbidden Fruit and will never give it up. She concedes to the fact that it will be just her and Baby Bear now. She will make a good life for him until Baby Bear grows a little bit older and leaves home to start a family of his own. Her heart hurts for Yobdab, and she misses him. The love she has for him is strong, there is no other that could fill her heart like him. What a terrible journey they took.

      Before the Forbidden Fruit, their lives where filled with laughter and love. The more he ate of the Forbidden Fruit the further away he became. Their laughter stopped, they played with Baby Bear no more and their beautiful, comfortable cave became dirty and looked abandoned. No, Mama Bear is right and now that she knows Baby Bear is alive, she has a second chance at life, she wants to live! She wants to breathe and she wants her Baby Bear back.

      Working her way up the mountain, each step gets harder and harder for Lrigdoog. Never being on the mountain before, she does not know the area and is

climbing the mountain out of instinct only.  Everything is going all right until she reaches a steep and jagged rock wall. She has no choice but to turn around and go back to find another way, or take a  chance and scale her way to the other side. Looking over the edge, Lrigdoog gets chills down her back, she knows that this is going to be very dangerous. The clouds have been hanging low, wrapping her in a thick mist, and it has been raining off and on for several days. The path is very scary. It is wet, slippery and narrow. "Can I do it?" she asks herself out loud. She decides to go on, because she knows that if she goes back, she will never make it to the top. "I must do this! I have no choice, my love for Baby Bear is my strength." she whispers. The rock is very sharp, cutting her paws with each step.

Slowly and carefully,  taking her time, hugging the cold, jagged ledge she moves one paw next to the other. One slip and Lrigdoog could fall hundreds of feet to the ground. Digging her already sore and bleeding claws deep into every crevice she can find, she grabs a hold of the rock, moving one small step at a time. It takes her half a day to make the journey across the sheer cliff, but she does make it. Exhausted, physically and mentally, she is into the fifth day of the most difficult time in her life. She is alone, she is sick, her paws are cut, and her swollen body is crying out for the Forbidden Fruit.

The rain continues pounding the ground she walks, and the path is muddy and  full of broken limbs and more sharp rocks. Moving at a faster pace, trying to make up for the time it took her to cross the ledge, things are looking much brighter until her back paws get caught on a tree limb, and she goes down stumbling, sliding to her knees, and flopping down onto her belly. Her front paws slide on the rocky ground beneath her, cutting them even more. She howls in pain and rolls on her side, laying where she has fallen. Sobbing she cries out, "I can't go on, I can't. I am not going to make it. I am sorry for the way that I have behaved … Oh,  Baby Bear, I am so, so sorry. Yobdab, where are you? oh, I wished you were here. I wished our life was like it was."

Laying her head on her bleeding paws, Lrigdoog feels that she cannot go another step, and she lies there crying for a long time. It would be so much easier for her to lie down and die.  At this moment, she would welcome that except … she realizes that the love she has for Baby Bear is much stronger than the desire to give up. Gathering all of her strength, she pulls herself up on all four injured paws and continues her journey to the top, each step more agonizing than the one before.

Two days later Lrigdoog walks out of the clouds and is standing high on the rim of Noitalosi looking down into a crater filled with paradise. The sun is shining brightly, and soft puffs of clouds hang high above the prettiest landscape she has ever seen. It is even more beautiful than Tserofniar.

Slowly, she makes her descent into the crater and is surrounded by giant blueberry bushes. Lrigdoog stops to eat some, and they are even more delicious than they look. She drinks from the stream, the juice of the earth is pure, cold, nourishing and healing. The cool water feels good on her injured paws and belly. When she finishes drinking Lrigdoog gets out of the stream and shakes, ever so gently and with each step that she takes into Noitalosi, she knows that her life is going to change. She knows it.

Lrigdoog's wounds heal fast, and she adjusts to her new environment quickly but, she is sick from not eating the Forbidden Fruit and her body and mind are playing tricks on her. She went through some very difficult times, but with the knowledge that her Baby Bear is a live, gives her hope. All she wants is her life back to normal.

She knows that she is the one in control of her life, not Yobdab. Just because he gave her the Forbidden Fruit didn't mean she had to indulge. She could have said "No" but she didn't. She took the fruit of her own free will and ate it, all of it!

With each day her attitude becomes refreshing and full of new desires. She loves being in Noitalosi learning to love life and herself with each new day. The evening skies are beautiful and filled with so many stars, that it feels as if she could almost reach up and pick them from the sky.

Eight months pass for Lrigdoog since she came to live in this part of the Cipmylo Forest, now she is completely clean of the Forbidden Fruit. Her black fur is shiny, thick, and soft. Her eyes are clear with sparkle, she can see life again. She has never looked so beautiful and felt so healthy in her whole life.

She wakes on a beautiful morning with the warm sun shining on her face, butterflies dancing from colorful flower to flower, birds chattering to each other as they partake of the luscious, wild blackberries, and bathes in the cool stream.

Lrigdoog stands on her hind legs and stretches her front paws into the air

and turns her head towards the blue sky. If she could only fly she would. Her spirit is so light and full of joy.

"Today is the day that I leave Noitalosi. I have reached my goal. I am no longer enslaved to the Forbidden Fruit, and I want to see my Baby Bear and Mama Bear. I am happy and ready to start a new life free of the Forbidden Fruit." As Lrigdoog speaks these truths into the wind, she walks to the stream to drink the juice of the earth and wash her face and paws. Then she strolls down the path to eat blueberries for her breakfast, knowing that she will have a long journey down the steep mountain. When she finishes eating she turns around, and looking at the beautiful valley that has been her home for so long, she takes a deep breath and whispers, "Thank you!" to all of the other animals that she has been living with for the past eight months, to Mother Earth for the beautiful space that allowed her to heal and to the Creator for giving her the strength to go on. Lrigdoog begins her journey to the top of the rim that will lead to her new life.

She stops and turns to view the valley one more time when she reaches the rim of Noitalosi. With spirit clean and a light heart, Lrigdoog stretches her paws open toward the valley, lifts her head toward the sun, and says, " I give thanks to you, Noitalosi, for allowing me to cleanse my spirit here and regain my life. So be it!" With her thanks given she turns around and starts her journey down the mountain.

Chapter 6
# The Reunion

It does not take as long to get down as it did to get to the top of Noitalosi. She makes the entire journey to the edge of Tserofniar in four days this time. She travels a different route going down the mountain, because this is a new beginning. Her travel is delightful, but she finds that she is a little bit nervous; after all Baby Bear has not seen her since he was three months old! Will he remember me?

Just outside of Tserofniar Lrigdoog runs into a huge field of Forbidden Fruit. She quickly thinks, should I travel the extra day and walk around so as not to be tempted? … NO! of course not. I am strong now, and I can do this! She heads straight through the field. The sweet smell is overwhelming, almost a drug in and of itself. She remembers the sweet taste of the Forbidden Fruit, and her mouth starts to water. It is so hard to walk past each bush without touching the berries; they are so plump, and there is no way to ignore them because their sparkle is so beautiful, and there are sooo many of them! Lrigdoog places a picture of Baby Bear in her mind, remembers the taste of the giant blueberries of Noitalosi, and breaks into a fast run.

When Lrigdoog nears Mama Bear's cave in Tserofniar, it is late afternoon, and the weather is sunny but cool. Mama Bear sees Lrigdoog right away and approaches her with great strength showing. Lrigdoog lowers her head down respectfully toward the ground. Mama Bear acknowledges her with a deep grunt, and Lrigdoog looks up into Mama Bear's eyes.

When Mama Bear sees Lrigdoog's eyes, she gasps in surprise. "Lrigdoog," she says, "you are beautiful!" Lrigdoog looks at Mama Bear with a shocked, but thankful look in her eyes, as Mama Bear continues, "Your eyes are clear … your fur is clean … you look healthy, and I can see that you have rid yourself of the Forbidden Fruit." In a shaken and emotional voice, Mama Bear says, "I am very proud of you."

Lrigdoog stands up, and Mama Bear steps forward and gives Lrigdoog a hug. Lrigdoog was not expecting Mama Bear to be so accepting because of her past behavior and the fact that she placed Baby Bear's life in jeopardy.

Where in the forest the tears came from, Lrigdoog doesn't know, but she

starts to cry uncontrollably. She is taken by surprise; it must have been all of the years, of being so lost, built up inside her. Mama Bear calms her down, telling her that everything will be fine now and that it is the future that they need to concentrate on, not the past. Mama Bear says " For if your head is cranked backwards how can you see what's in front of you?"

It takes Lrigdoog a few minutes to regain her composure, and finally, she says to Mama Bear, "Thank you for sending me away and making me realize what I had done to my life. But most of all, thank you for raising Baby Bear and taking good care of him. I will be indebted to you for the rest of my life, Mama Bear."

"No, do not be indebted to me," Mama Bear says to Lrigdoog in a gentle voice. "Be proud of yourself and make the rest of your life the happiest for you and Baby Bear."

"Thank you," whispers Lrigdoog, "I will."

Then Mama Bear finally utters the words that Lrigdoog has waited so long to hear, "Come, let's go see Baby Bear." Lrigdoog is excited but nervous; she wipes her tear stained face and follows Mama Bear.

Baby Bear is in the river when Mama Bear and Lrigdoog arrive; he is pulling his huge, boxy, head out from under the water with a big salmon clenched in his jaws. Standing on his hind legs, water flies through the air, and the salmon is twisting vigorously, trying to get away. He sees Mama Bear, and another bear that he does not recognize, walking up the path towards him. Lrigdoog is impressed with his size. She sees that he has grown into a huge boar of a bear (just like Mama Bear knew he would).

A feeling inside Baby Bear tells him to let go of his catch and come out of the water to meet the two bears, so he does. The grateful salmon swims away with a splash. Parting the waters with his huge body, Baby Bear steps out and shakes the water off. Even standing on all four paws, he towers above both Mama Bear and Lrigdoog. Baby Bear senses a vague memory when he comes face to face with the

bear standing next to Mama Bear, but he is not sure who she is. Yet, as he sniffs the air, he seems to recognize a familiar fragrance from her.

Although she has a deep fear of being rejected, Lrigdoog walks up to Baby Bear without hesitation and looks up into his eyes. She says, "Baby Bear, I am Lrigdoog your … your mother." Lrigdoog waits, for what seems like an eternity, for Baby Bear to say something. Mama Bear stands in silence and knows that she is watching the future unfold for all of them.

Baby Bear cocks his head, never letting his eyes leave Lrigdoog's, and softly whispers, "You are my mother?" Slowly, he then turns his head and looks to Mama Bear for guidance. Mama Bear's big brown eyes look lovingly at Baby Bear. He sees a twinkle in them and a look of approval. She nods her head sending Baby Bear a message of love and assurance. He turns back to Lrigdoog and opens his front paws to hug her. Lrigdoog is relieved and crying as she hugs Baby Bear for the first time in three years.

Mama Bear also cries as she watches Lrigdoog and Baby Bear hug. In her mind there are a hundred thoughts: Oh no, what's going to happen now? Will Baby Bear be gone from me? I will miss him so much. What will life be like without him? Will Lrigdoog stay off the Forbidden Fruit? These are all unsettling issues that Mama Bear never thought that she would have to deal with. She thought that Baby Bear would be with her until he grew old enough to go out on his own and create his own den and new life. Her heart pounds … it is the sound of mourning, a deep drum beating in pain; quietly her heart breaks.

Lrigdoog stays with Mama Bear and Baby Bear for three months, getting reacquainted. Mama Bear is happy to have Lrigdoog back in their lives, and she enjoys watching Lrigdoog and Baby Bear run and wrestle on the soft moss. Mama Bear is getting old and tired and cannot play with Baby Bear the way that she used to. In fact, it hurts to romp with him sometimes, but she does it because she loves Baby Bear, and because she does not think about age until her bones and muscles ache at the end of the day or the next morning when she wakes and tries to get

up. Oh, I do hurt, she says to herself at those times. I just can't run as fast, or climb as far, as I used to. Time is catching up with her, she feels it more and more each day, and she sees how good it is for Lrigdoog to have come back. Now, Lrigdoog can do the things with Baby Bear that have become difficult for her to do.

At the end of three months, Lrigdoog approaches Mama Bear down by the river and says, "Mama Bear, I need to talk with you?"

Mama Bear looks up, into Lrigdoog's face and she already knows what she is going to say, her heart skips a beat. "Yes, Lrigdoog," Mama Bear says, with a deep, knowing sigh, "I knew that this day would come."

"Mama Bear, you have been a wonderful influence in both Baby Bear's life and in mine," Lrigdoog quietly continues. "I owe you my life for making me realize that I needed to turn it around and for raising Baby Bear. But I feel that the time has come for us to leave and to build a new home for ourselves. Baby Bear will have but a year or so before he leaves the den for good, and I think that it would be good for us to have that time on our own. It is something I missed because of my behavior and now have a second chance, I hope you understand?"

Mama Bear agrees, "Yes, Lrigdoog, you are right. You and Baby Bear should experience being together in a home of your own before he grows up and leaves". Mama Bear tries to make light of the conversation, trying not to show the hurt that is building from within her spirit. "Where will you be going?"

Having already come up with a plan, Lrigdoog says, "I think that we will go back to the West End. There are plenty of fresh berries there and several springs and creeks. The vegetation is lush and we will be far enough away from Skrof that we will not need to worry about other animals coming into the area to eat the Forbidden Fruit; all of the bushes there have been picked and destroyed by careless animals."

"Yes, this sounds like a good plan, When will you leave?"

"Well, I was thinking that we would leave tomorrow. Will that be all right with you?"

"Yes, of course it will be, Lrigdoog. The decision is yours," Mama Bear says, trying to hide the sadness in her smile.

"Will you be all right by yourself, Mama Bear?" Lrigdoog asks. She cares deeply for Mama Bear and knows that she is used to having Baby Bear with her.

"Oh, yes, I will be fine," she assures her. "With the spring months approaching and the worst of winter behind us, I am going to indulge on late blackberries, red huckleberries, and relax. I'll be fine. You and Baby Bear can come and visit me anytime you want, and I will sometimes make the trip to see you. My bones are starting to ache a little, and I will not be doing much traveling, but I will visit occasionally."

"Thank you, Mama Bear," says Lrigdoog. "I'll go and tell Baby Bear. I do love you!"

"I love you, too," says Mama Bear, and she slowly sits down as Lrigdoog leaves. A look of pain crosses Mama Bear face, she shakes her head and tears well up in her eyes as she takes in a deep breath. She knew this day was coming, but that does not ease the thought of not having Baby Bear around and the pain in her heart. She cannot help but worry about him … Will he be all right? Will Lrigdoog stay away from the forbidden fruit? She slumps further down as these thoughts crosses her mind. Oh, what a sick feeling she has.

That night Baby Bear finds Mama Bear on the other side of the lake by the falls. He tells her hello and that he has been looking for her. Responding, she says, "Yes, I have been here for a while."

Baby Bear walks over and gives Mama Bear a kiss and sits next to her. "Mama Bear, you have been all I know," he says, looking deep into her eyes. "Throughout my life you have been my teacher, my playmate, my protector, and my family. You gave me a beautiful den to live in, and you always made me laugh. Leaving you is a hard thing for me to do, and I worry about you."

Mama Bear touches Baby Bear's furry face and looks into his eyes with her soft, deep brown eyes and says, "We have had a wonderful time together. You have brought me such joy and kept me feeling young. To watch you grow from a baby bear into the sensitive, smart, strong, and handsome bear that you are today makes me very proud. Do not worry about me, Baby Bear, I will be fine. The Creator has seen to it that you and Lrigdoog have a second chance. It is time you go with your mother."

Holding back tears, Mama Bear gives Baby Bear a tight hug and kiss. But Baby Bear cannot hold back his tears as he hugs Mama Bear back. Then he gets up to leave and tells her, "I will miss you, but I will come to see you often. I love you, Mama Bear."

"Yes, I love you, too, Baby Bear," she whispers as she watches Baby Bear walk out of sight. She feels such strong pain in her heart, and when she see's that he is gone she lets her tears fall. Her life is going to change without Baby Bear. This, she was not expecting.

Early the next morning Lrigdoog and Baby Bear get ready to leave. Mama Bear tells Lrigdoog, "Take care of yourself and know, that in thought and in spirit, I will be with you at all times." Then she turns to Baby Bear and says, "Remember the life lessons that you have learned in your time here, remember to follow your intuition Baby Bear and know that you are but a thought away from me. Don't forget to count the stars and let the wind kiss your face"

"Oh, yes, Mama Bear, I will never forget all that you have taught me, especially, to count the stars in the evening sky, to wave to the moon, and to send a thought to the sun. I have also learned to look into other animals' eyes when I speak and when they speak to me. I will remember it all, Mama Bear. And most of all, I will remember you. I will never forget you, and I will come to see you often, I promise."

With this, Mama Bear and Baby Bear hug and say their good byes and I love you's. Mama Bear watches as they walk away, down the path into the forest.

She knew that this was going to happen, but didn't think about how it was going to feel. Again tears drop as the feeling of emptiness engulfs her. As Lrigdoog and Baby Bear disappear into the trees, the beautiful Tserofniar forest suddenly becomes quiet and lonely. The only sound that Mama Bear can hear is the drum beat of her own heart. She has never known such pain.

Lrigdoog and Baby Bear make the journey to the West End in three days. They find a cave and set up home, filling it with cedar boughs, leaves, and what little moss that they can find, for the moss does not grow as thick and luscious here

as it does in Tserofniar. Making the move with his mother is not as easy as Baby Bear thought it would be.

His life with Mama Bear had been so sweet. Although Mama Bear taught him many lessons and was strict, she treated him special, giving him all of her attention and affection. Lrigdoog tries her best to make their new home as comfortable as possible, but the living conditions are not as nice here as they were in Tserofniar: the moss is not as green and thick and curly, and the creek, unlike the lake, is not big and full of fish.

Baby Bear also finds that it is not easy making new friends here. Most of the other animals' lives are affected by the Forbidden Fruit in some way or another; either their parents are eating the fruit or the younger animals themselves have begun eating it. Lrigdoog keeps a close eye on him, still trusting his good judgment but not wanting him to associate with the wrong animals. He misses his friends in Tserofniar, Flagtail and Buttercup and Wapiti, especially. He doubts that he will ever be able to find friends here who are as good. This makes Baby Bear even more homesick for Tserofniar, and he misses Mama Bear terribly.

After a month of getting settled in, Baby Bear tells his mother how much he misses Mama Bear and that he wants to go see her. Worried about him traveling alone, Lrigdoog tells Baby Bear to be very careful on his journey. Baby Bear tells his mother to also be safe and to take good care of herself while he is gone. Baby Bear kisses Lrigdoog and leaves for Tserofniar, traveling, for the first time, alone.

The closer Baby Bear gets to Mama Bear, the prettier the forest becomes. There's no place like Tserofniar, and his heart grows happier with anticipation with each step. Along the way, he sends messages with the bluebirds to Mama Bear, and they tell her of his journey to see her.

Mama Bear is thrilled to hear that Baby Bear is on his way to see her, she has missed him more than words can describe. When he arrives, they hug and hug. Mama Bears face rubs against his and she takes a deep breath of his scent. "Oh, how I missed you," she tells him. They speak to one another as if they had never

been apart. Baby Bear tells her about his new home and what it is like for him there. She sees a look on his face that she has never seen before and can tell that things, at times, have been difficult. She is concerned and wishes that he had never left, but she does not tell Baby Bear this. Mama Bear knows that everything changes; she is just happy that he is here with her now.

They fish together for dinner and sleep well that night. Baby Bear never thought that his old bed could feel more comfortable than it did when he was living here, but it does. When he gets snuggled in he tells Mama Bear "On your mark!" Mama Bear laughs and says "Get set!" and they both yell "Sleep!" It is the deepest sleep he has had in the last month.

Baby Bear stays for five days with Mama Bear, every day filled with warm laughter and more of Mama Bear's "life's learning lessons." Mama Bear tells him " You can take a question you have and ask ten different animals the same question and you will get ten different answers. Always try to answer your own question, and if you can not, you come see Mama Bear." They both laugh. He spent time with his friends Buttercup, Flagtail, and Wapiti. They splash in the lake and also spend an afternoon lying under the old crabapple tree in the open field with some of their other animal friends talking like they used to. How they all miss Baby Bear. He tells them how different it is in the West End and how good they have it right here. They said they would come and see him soon.

When Baby Bear leaves, he is sad to go but returns to the West End with his heart filled with joy from being with Mama Bear and his friends. When he arrives he finds Lrigdoog cleaning the den, and she is very happy to see him. She asks him about his journey and about Mama Bear. He tells her all that they did. Lrigdoog listens with a pang of jealousy; she knows of the special bond that Baby Bear and Mama Bear will always have. She is truly grateful for this but also wishes that she and Baby Bear could have that kind of bond. She tells herself that it is something that she will have to work on and that, in time, it will happen.

## Chapter 7

# How Things Can Change

In the town of Skrof Yobdab, Elbuort, and Regnad have become completely different bears than when they were captured. Once again, they are fat, their fur is clean, and there is a sparkle that shines in their clear eyes. Their attitudes have completely changed, and they are bears who are now nice and very grateful.

The town's people are happy and proud of themselves for all that they accomplished in getting the bears clean and off of the Sgurd Berry, and the day has come for them to be released. The man, who first spoke to the bears through the window on that first day, is the man who comes to let them go. He wishes them well and opens the bolted doors. The bears, without hesitation, run out into the open air and to freedom. As they run, the man watches their thick, shiny fur rippling across their fat bodies.

As Elbuort and Regnad run on ahead, Yobdab stops and looks back at the building that they were held in for so long. Then, he looks into the eyes of the man who set them free, and gives him a look that says, Thank you! The man understands this, and nods his head. Yobdab turns and goes to catch up with his friends.

When the three of them enter the forest, after leaving town, they soon run into a bush of the Forbidden Fruit. Yobdab looks at Elbuort and Regnad, and they stare at the fruit, causing them to flash back in time. Yobdab is the first to break the silence, and he blurts out, "I am going to look for Lrigdoog and help her get off the Forbidden Fruit. I want a good life, and I don't want anything more to do with the Forbidden Fruit!"

Regnad and Elbuort both agree and vow at the same time, "Right … we're not eating it either! We have learned our lesson." The three of them say goodbye and wish each other luck. "We'll see each other again. Take care of yourselves," Yobdab says, leaving his friends and walking on into the forest in search of Lrigdoog. As he turns back, to take one last look at his friends leaving, he sees Elbuort reach into the Forbidden Fruit bush and pick a berry.

Yobdab shakes his head in disbelief and turns around to continue his journey, knowing that Elbuort did not see him look back. Yobdab knows that he

cannot do anything about somebody else wanting to partake of the Forbidden Fruit. Elbuort is the creator of his own life, and he will live it the way that he wants. But Yobdab has a wife to find and a life to put back together, He continues, with new confidence to walk his path.

After days of searching for Lrigdoog, Yobdab has no luck in finding her. He is very worried that something horrible may have happened to her while he was captured in Skrof. Stopping for a moment exhausted and almost near tears wanting to know where his beautiful Lrigdoog is. He hears noise above the trees. Looking up to see it is the bluebirds, he calls out, "Have you seen Lrigdoog?"

When the bluebirds look down to see who is speaking to them, they are amazed at what they see. Yobdab thought that he could actually see skid marks in the sky; they put their brakes on so fast in mid-flight. They could not believe their eyes, "Yobdab! Is that you?" "Yes," he answers.

The bluebirds see how clean and fat Yobdab looks and realize that he is no longer partaking of the Forbidden Fruit. They happily chirp and fly down to where he is standing, "Lrigdoog and Baby Bear are living in the West End."

Yobdab is shocked, and goose bumps cover his entire body! "Did you say Baby Bear is with Lrigdoog?" he asks, in disbelief. "Yes, and they are doing well," the birds happily reply.

Taken with emotion, Yobdab sits down on a log. Shaking his head in disbelief he can feel a stinging sensation in his eyes and nose as tears well up. Placing his paws over his face he cries. "My Baby Bear is alive and with my Lrigdoog! Oh … thank you Creator! Thank you!" he speaks out to the sky as he sobs. With great joy filling his heart, and a feeling of new strength, he regains his composure, gives thanks to the bluebirds, who are perched on the tree limb above and he sets out in a full run toward the West End.

Baby Bear and Lrigdoog are playing and laughing aloud in the creek that is near their cave when Baby Bear suddenly hears someone approaching in the woods. He instantly goes into danger alert, and Lrigdoog does the same when she hears the alarming sounds after Baby Bear alerted her. She stands next to Baby Bear. They are back-to-back, ready to fight whomever it is that is breaking branches and racing through the woods. As the noise grows louder and closer, Baby Bear lets go a deep, ear-shattering growl that stops whom ever it is in his or her tracks. Both Baby Bear and Lrigdoog stand motionless and listen. They hold their breath and in the silence can hear a leaf fall to the ground and the beat of their own drum pounding in their chest.

Out of the forest they hear their names called, "Lrigdoog, Baby Bear, it is me … its Yobdab!"

Lrigdoog cannot believe her ears, and she is overwhelmed with emotion at the sound of her Yobdab's voice. She gasps in awe. But in that very second she has to share fear with her joyful emotions. She is afraid, because he partakes of the Forbidden Fruit. She does not move and whispers to Baby Bear to stay still. Then, Yobdab steps out of the woods, and she sees him.

Her eyes begin to tear, she sees how clean, fat and handsome he is. He is so happy to see them! He sees that she is also clean of the Forbidden Fruit, and Baby Bear quickly realizes that this is his father.

Yobdab slowly approaches his wife and son, nearly in shock seeing Baby Bear … alive! … and Lrigdoog clean, beautiful, and healthy; all three of them hug one another.

Yobdab is so happy that they are all back together and that they are safe. He is amazed at how big and strong Baby Bear is and so proud of Lrigdoog for cleansing herself of the Forbidden Fruit. How things can change.

## Chapter 8

# The Broken Promise

Together again, Yobdab, Lrigdoog, and Baby Bear settle in as a family. Over the coming months they get to know one another again, and Baby Bear continues the journey to visit Mama Bear. He let's Mama Bear know right away that his father has come back, and that he is clean of the Forbidden Fruit. Mama Bear is elated, she always liked Yobdab and gives thanks to the Creator for the turn of events.

Each time Baby Bear visits her he takes pride in doing things for her, like cleaning out the den, picking berries, patrolling Tserofniar for any unwanted Forbidden Fruit bushes and catching fish.

Baby Bear notices, as time goes by, how slow Mama Bear has become. She grunts sometimes when getting up, and it seems as if her eyesight is not as keen as it use to be. She also seems to be forgetting things. Baby Bear can no longer help but notice these things; they are so obvious. He even sees that Mama Bear has grown a few gray whiskers around her mouth and chin. Seeing her age brings a new emotions to Baby Bear; he is more concerned for her welfare and becomes even more protective and caring for her.

They have talked about the passing, called death. Mama Bear has explained that the spirit that lives in the center of our bodies is our light being. We are the creation and product of the Creator, and without the presence of our light being, our bear bodies would not work. When our light being does leave our body, the body dies and our spirit goes on to another adventure. It goes home to the Creator. Mama Bear says " Know My spirit will always be with you. Know Baby Bear that you are never alone and are always loved."

One day, while at home fishing in the creek with his mother and father, Baby Bear walks out of the water with a fish in his mouth. He gets a sick feeling in the pit

**49**

of his stomach. A shiver runs up his spine. Standing up on his hind legs, placing his paws over his stomach, and a look of horror crosses his face.

Lrigdoog looks up and sees how strange Baby Bear looks. She asks him, "What's wrong?" He doesn't quite know how to answer, and she has to yell at him again, "What's wrong!?"

Baby Bear looks at Lrigdoog, drops the fish from his mouth, and whispers to her, "Something is wrong, I have to go see Mama Bear right away! I have to go NOW!"

Baby Bear runs past his parents as fast as he can, and they yell, "Do you want us to go with you?" But he is gone too quickly for them to hear his answer. Lrigdoog tells Yobdab that they must follow him to make certain that everything is all right.

Baby Bear makes the four-day journey in two days. Luckily, it is the time of the full moon and the skies are clear, allowing Grandmother Moon to guide his way through the evening.

Exhausted when he reaches Mama Bear's cave, his feelings are confirmed; Mama Bear is lying on her left side next to the old growth cedar tree outside her cave. She is very sick, so sick that when she hears someone coming she cannot get up and doesn't even care who it is. Thank goodness, she realizes, it is Baby Bear.

"Oh, Mama Bear, what's the matter," Baby Bear cries, as he kneels down beside her. She opens her eyes to see Baby Bear, and in a very soft voice, struggling for air, Mama Bear says, "Oh … Baby Bear … you are here. You heard me calling you. I … so wanted to see you … one more time."

"Yes, Mama Bear," he answers her in a desperate voice, "I am here. I heard you calling. What can I do? What's wrong with you?"

Mama Bear confesses, "All of a sudden I became sick … I don't know what happened, but I do know that my time here … is finished. I feel my spirit wants to leave." Baby Bear cannot believe what he is hearing. He whispers, "No, Mama Bear, no..."

"Remember all you have learned, Baby Bear," she tells him in a soft voice. "Remember to love … and to love yourself. Remember … that I love you.""No! Don't go!" Baby Bear is almost screaming. Mama Bear looks into his eyes and gently whispers, "Know that I will be … I will always be with you."

Baby Bear pleads, "No, Mama Bear! No, don't you leave me. I need you. Please … let me stay with you, and I will take care of you, I promise. Please, Mama Bear … don't go!" But as Baby Bear says these last words, Mama Bear takes her last breath. A burst of wind passes through Baby Bear as he gasps with surprise. For a split second he is engulfed with a flash of beautiful light. Mama Bear's head falls heavy in Baby Bear's paws and she is silent. He realizes that her spirit has left her body.

Not believing this is happening, Baby Bear is in a state of shock, he has never experienced the death of a loved one before, not in this way. For a long time he thought that his parents were dead, but he barely remembered them, and they did not die in his arms. Everything fell silent. The birds stopped singing, and the wind stood still. The only sound that Baby Bear thought he could hear is the beat of a distant drum, it is his heart breaking.

Baby Bear gently places Mama Bear's head on the ground, gently rubs her face and stands up. With every ounce of energy that is left him, he belts out a roar that comes from deep within; a cry that is heard throughout Tserofniar. Baby Bear falls again to his knees and then to his front paws, sobbing her name over and over, "Mama Bear, Mama Bear, how could this happen? I'm lost … oh, I am so lost."

He cries deep, earth-shaking sobs for a long time, not wanting to believe that his Mama Bear's life is no more. Completely exhausted, he lifts his tear stained face towards the heavens, as if looking for an answer from the Creator … but before his tear-filled eyes could reach the sky, they are distracted by the reflection of a sparkle in a teardrop that begins to fall from one eye.

In front of him is the Mother Lode of all the Forbidden Fruit bushes that Mama Bear planted many years ago, with one huge berry, dangling inches in front of him. Baby Bear slowly reaches into the bush and picks the berry from the limb of the Forbidden Berry bush. The berry willingly drops into his paw. Another tear falls from his eye, feeling the strong emotions from his broken spirit as he stares at

the Forbidden Fruit laying in the middle of his paw ... his intuition is whispering to him that this berry is the cause for all wrong doings in the Cipmylo forest, however, it seems to ease the other animals pain. A cool breeze suddenly wraps around him sending a chill right through his being and he can hear Mama Bear's voice whisper "Oh no ... Baby Bear."

Linda Silvas "Little Tree" was born and raised in San Diego and heritage is of the Juaneno Band of Mission Indians, Acjachemen located on the Southern California Coast.

In 1989 she relocated to the Pacific Northwest where she resides in a log home in Sequim, Washington.

Her studio is located at the base of the Olympic Mountains (the "Cipmylo" Forest) where she writes, produces her own line of drums, original art and is also a weaver of the pine needle.

As an international speaker, Linda uses "Mama Bear Baby Bear" as the base of her presentation, her quest is to educate about the dangers of substance abuse.

She is strong in her commitment to keeping the traditions of the native way alive.

Linda gave birth to the story of "Mama Bear Baby Bear" through her own personal experience, which led to a magical, spiritual, journey that has become so much more than just one book, more than just one story…for she believes that "We are all the connection in a full circle, the circle never ends".

Our thoughts ride the wind.

Linda Silvas, "Little Tree"

**Mama Bear Baby Bear** Book

*Mama Bear Baby Bear* Logo Drum

*Mama Bear Baby Bear* Moon Drum

*Mama Bear Baby Bear* Special Edition
Cover *(top left)* and Inside *(top right)*

**Mama Bear Baby Bear** T-shirts
They come in black logo on red t-shirt or White logo on black t-shirt.

*Mama Bear Baby Bear* Stocking Pair

*Mama Bear Baby Bear* Pillow

*Mama Bear Baby Bear* Apron Pair

# Mama Bear Baby Bear ORDER FORM

| | Quanty | Size | Color | Cost | T otal |
|---|---|---|---|---|---|
| **Mama Bear Baby Bear Book** <br> Bulk discounts for *Mama Bear Baby Bear* books are available. Write or call for information. Toll-Free 1(888) 224-7039. Email: ltcreate@olypen.com. Website: www.mamabearbabybear.com **$24** | | | | $24 | |
| **Mama Bear Baby Bear T-Shirts** <br> 100% cotton. **Available in XS / LG / XL / XXL.** <br> **BLACK** t-shirt with red logo. **RED** t-shirt with black logo. **$23** | | | | $23 | |
| **Mama Bear Baby Bear Drum** <br> 16" hand drum up to 36" double sided Buffalo Pow Wow Drum. Drums are designed by Linda Silvas "Little Tree", handmade with Elk and Buffalo. The back of drum is finished with Elk Fur, Bear Fur or Deer Tail. Each Drum comes with a beater that matches the back design of Drum."Mama Bear Baby Bear" design is painted on Drumhead. No design is a like, each drum is signed and numbered. **Choose Logo Design or Moon Design. $200 and up** | | | | CALL | |
| **Mama Bear Baby Bear Matching Aprons with logo** <br> Hand made by Designer Caroline Carnathan. Matching Aprons are made to fit adult and child. Good cooking in Mama Bear's kitchen! **$45 per matching pair** | | | | $45 | |
| **Mama Bear Baby Bear Dream Pillows** <br> Stuffed with herbs found in Tserofniar, Home of Mama Bear Baby Bear in the Cipmylo Forest. **$12** | | | | $12 | |
| **Mama Bear Baby Bear Matching Stockings** <br> Handmade of soft buckskin and trimmed with Elk Fur, Bear Fur or Lamb Fur. **$150 per matching pair** | | | | $150 | |
| **Special Edition Book** of **Mama Bear Baby Bear** <br> Book is handmade with real tree bark with the name "Mama Bear Baby Bear" burned onto front cover, spine of book is laced with bear fur, feathers and deer tail. Inside is covered with soft buckskin and story is printed on parchment paper. Each book is numbered and signed. **$400** | | | | $400 | |

|  | |
|---|---|
| Sub-total | |
| Washington State residents add applicable sales tax: | |
| Shipping | |
| TOTAL | |

***Most items in-stock can be shipped next day.***

We charge for shipping because we have no choice. But we will not charge for handling because we, **Mama Bear Baby Bear**, are honored that you want our product. When placing an order, we can e-mail or call to provide shipping cost. Please contact us. Phone: (888) 224-7039, Email: ltcreate@olypen.com

❑ Check enclosed made payable to **Little Tree Creations**
❑ VISA    ❑ MasterCard    ❑ AMEX    ❑ Dinners

_____ — _____ — _____ / _____
CARD #                                          EXP. DATE

_____
SIGNATURE

**Mama Bear Baby Bear**
PO Box 178
Carlsborg, WA 98324

Name _____

Business (if applicable) _____

Address _____

City _____ ST _____ Zip _____

Country _____ Phone (for delivery) _____

E-mail _____

# YES ❑ please contact me with news or upcoming events

Mama Bear Baby Bear
PO Box 178
Carlsborg, WA 98324

Please fold and secure at top with tape.

Please fold and secure at top with tape.

# Send a letter to Mama Bear or Baby Bear

Let us know how you're doing, we will write back.

**Be sure to include your address and e-mail and we will keep you informed of Mama Bear Baby Bear events.**

Mailing address
Mama Bear Baby Bear
PO Box 178
Carlsborg, WA 98324
1 888 224 7039
www.mamabearbabybear.com

**Mama Bear Baby Bear**
**PO Box 178**
**Carlsborg, WA 98324**

Please fold and secure at top with tape.

Please fold and secure at top with tape.